Romans, Saxons & Vikings

Beliefs and Myths of Anglo-Saxon England

Martyn Whittock

First published in Great Britain by
Heinemann Library,
Halley Court, Jordan Hill, Oxford OX2 8EJ
a division of Reed Educational & Professional Publishing Ltd.

OXFORD FLORENCE PRAGUE MADRID
ATHENS MELBOURNE AUCKLAND
KUALA LUMPUR SINGAPORE TOKYO
IBADAN NAIROBI KAMPALA
JOHANNESBURG GABORONE
PORTSMOUTH NH (USA) CHICAGO
MEXICO CITY SAO PAULO

Designed by Ken Vail Graphic Design

Produced by Celia Floyd

Illustrations by Jeff Edwards

Originated by Magnet Harlequin Group

Printed in Great Britain by
Bath Press Colourbooks, Glasgow

01 00 99 98 97

10 9 8 7 6 5 4 3 2 1

ISBN 0 431 05980 2

British Library Cataloguing in Publication Data

Whittock, Martyn J. (Martyn John)
Beliefs and myths of Anglo-Saxon England
1.Mythology, English – Juvenile literature
2.Legends – England – Juvenile literature
I.Title II.Anglo-Saxon England
398'.0942

Acknowledgements

The Publishers would like to thank the following
for permission to reproduce photographs.

Barnaby's Picture Library/John Beecham: p. 19 ○
British Museum Trustees: pp. 4, 7, 17, 26 ○ British
Museum/Archives of the Dept of Mediaeval and
Later Antiquities, photo Miss B Wagstaff ARPS:
p. 21 ○ Corpus Christi College Cambridge, Parker
Library: p. 13 ○ Dean and Chapter of Durham
Cathedral: p. 24 ○ English Heritage: p. 7 ○ Robert
Estall Photographs: pp. 11, 19, 23 (left)

○ Oxford Archaeological Unit: p. 29 ○
Oxford Institute of Archaeology: p. 5
(top) ○ Norfolk Museums Service/Mick
Sharp: p. 5 (bottom) ○ Norfolk
Museums Service/Michael Dabski: p.9
○ Photoresources/C.M. Dixon: p. 27 ○
Rouen Bibliothèque Municipale/
D. Tragin/C. Lancien: p. 25

Cover photograph, reproduced with
permission of Rouen Bibliothèque
Municipale, shows the Descent of the
Holy Spirit at Pentecost.

Our thanks to Keith Stringer, of the
Department of History at Lancaster
University, for his comments in the
preparation of this book.

We would like to thank the following
Wiltshire schools for valuable
comments made regarding the
content and layout of this series:
Fitzmaurice Primary School,
Bradford-on-Avon; Dauntsey's
Primary School, West Lavington;
and Studley Green Primary School,
Trowbridge.

Details of written sources

D. M. Wilson (ed.), *The Northern
World,* Thames and Hudson 1980:
pp. 4B, 6AB, 8A, 10BD ○ L. Sherley-
Price (trans), *Bede's History of the
English Church and People*, Penguin
1968: pp. 5D, 13C, 18A, 20A, 21C ○
C. Fell, *Women in Anglo-Saxon
England*, Brit. Mus. Press 1984: p. 8B,
16A ○ P. Hunter-Blair, *Anglo-Saxon
England*, Cambridge University Press
1956: p. 9C ○ M. Whittock, *The
Origins of England AD410–600*, Croom
Helm 1986: pp. 10C, 26A ○ B. Yorke,
Wessex in the Early Middle Ages,
Leicester University Press 1995:
p. 14A, 16BC ○ J. Morris, *The Age
of Arthur*, Phillimore 1977: p. 14C ○
H. Mays-Harting, *The Coming of
Christianity to Anglo-Saxon England*,
Batsford 1991: p. 22B

For Florence, Jake and Isabelle Grigsby.

Contents

Clues about Anglo-Saxon beliefs

Many kinds of clues survive about Anglo-Saxon beliefs. But they are only clues, since people did not write down how they thought and felt in those days. Most of the evidence for people's beliefs comes from graves. This can sometimes be hard to piece together.

The first Anglo-Saxons came to Britain in the fifth century AD. They were not Christians. They **worshipped** many different gods. People like this were called **pagans** by the early Christians.

Some of the **British** people already living here were pagans too but some British had become Christians towards the end of the Roman Empire. From about AD600 the pagan Anglo-Saxons and the remaining British pagans gradually became Christians.

Changing clues about beliefs

There are not a lot of clues about the gods of the early pagan Anglo-Saxons. Later Christians did not want to record things about them. They thought they were bad. We know more about the Christian beliefs of the Anglo-Saxons than about the pagan ones.

Mixed clues about the gods

After AD789 **Viking** raiders invaded Britain. They were pagans too. Their gods were very like the old Anglo-Saxon gods. The clues they left make it hard to tell the difference between the Viking gods and the Anglo-Saxon gods.

Source A

*An Anglo-Saxon pot from about AD500. It is full of **cremated** human bones.*

Source B

Woden, that name means fury.

Adam of Bremen wrote this in the 12th century. Bremen is in Germany, so he may have got his ideas about Woden from the Viking people.

Source C

A buckle found in a grave at Finglesham, Kent. The figure holding two spears is probably the pagan god Woden. Can we assume that the person who wore this buckle was a follower of Woden?

Source E

A statue from a grave of the sixth century AD. It may be the lid of a cremation pot, but it is the only one like it to have been found so far. Is it the statue of a god? It is hard to be sure.

Source D

Some are still being snatched from the devil. Christian churches are being set up in places where some still **worship idols**.

Written by a Christian Anglo-Saxon, named Bede. He died in about AD735. He is describing people giving up their pagan beliefs.

The two chief gods

The two main Anglo-Saxon pagan gods were named Woden and Thunor.

Woden

Woden was one of the two chief pagan gods. He was particularly popular with Anglo-Saxon warriors and rulers. Many believed that he was their **ancestor**, who had once been a real person. But this is not so.

The Anglo-Saxons named Wednesday after Woden. This name means Woden's day. Woden was a warrior god. He was the god who looked after the borders between different kingdoms. He had power over animals like snakes, and could protect his followers from them.

Thunor

Thunor was a god popular with ordinary pagan Anglo-Saxons. Some of them thought he was more important than Woden.

The Anglo-Saxons named Thursday after Thunor. This means 'Thunor's day'. It was thought Thunor controlled the weather. His name means 'thunder'. His sign was the swastika (a cross with hooked ends). Some people put this sign on pots containing cremated bodies.

Source A

Woden, a king of the **barbarians**. After his death the pagans honoured him as a god. They offered him **sacrifices** in order to win battles, or to be brave.

Ethelweard, a Christian Anglo-Saxon, wrote this. He wrote in the late tenth century AD.

Source B

A snake came crawling, it killed nothing. For Woden took nine twigs. He struck the adder. It broke into nine parts.

*An Anglo-Saxon **charm** to protect people from harm.*

Source C

The Wansdyke in Wiltshire. Wansdyke means 'Woden's Dyke'. It was an Anglo-Saxon border in the sixth century AD.

How do we know?

Source A shows that some Anglo-Saxons thought Woden had once been a real person. Source B shows his power over snakes. Source C shows his name was linked to borders between kingdoms.

Source D shows the sign of Thunor. It shows he was thought to protect dead people.

Source D

A sixth century AD cremation pot from Norfolk. It has Thunor's sign of a swastika on it.

Other gods and goddesses

Woden and Thunor were the two main Anglo-Saxon gods. But other gods and goddesses were worshipped by the pagan Anglo-Saxons too.

There are not many clues about these other pagan gods and goddesses.

Tiw, the god of war

Tuesday was named after him. It means 'Tiw's day'. In Warwickshire there is a place named Tysoe. It means 'Tiw's hill'. There used to be a red horse cut in the hillside here. Perhaps it was a sign of Tiw. Perhaps a battle was fought here. We can only guess.

Another sign of Tiw was shaped like an arrow. This sign was an Anglo-Saxon rune. Runes were letters used for writing. This rune was named after Tiw. Sometimes we find it on **cremation** pots. One, in Norfolk, also had Tiw's name written on it.

Source B

Earth Mother, may God give her fertility. Grow crops, barley, the white wheat. All the fruits of the land.

An Anglo-Saxon charm to make land grow crops. It is from the eleventh century AD.

Source A

On the third day [Tuesday] they honour Mars, their battle god.

An Anglo-Saxon Christian, named Elfric, wrote this in the eleventh century AD. He meant the god Tiw, who was like the Roman war-god, Mars.

Source C

The third and fourth months were called after two goddesses Hretha and Eostre.

Written by the Christian Anglo-Saxon Bede. He died in AD735.

Pagan gods and goddesses of the earth

Anglo-Saxons also **worshipped** Mother Earth. She was thought to make the crops grow. Sometimes she was given the name Eostre, the goddess of Spring. Our modern word 'Easter' is from this name.

Lists of Wessex kings include one named Sceaf (meaning **sheaf**) and one named Beaw (meaning grain). Their names suggest that these were not kings at all, but old gods.

Anglo-Saxons also worshipped a goddess called Hretha. But all we know about her is her name. Friday was named after a goddess of love, whom the **Vikings** later knew as Frigg. Wyrd (Destiny) had control over people's lives.

How do we know?

Source A shows that Tiw was a war god, like the Roman god Mars. Source E shows the god's name on a pot. Perhaps it was meant to protect the dead person. Source B shows that later Anglo-Saxons still remembered a pagan goddess of the land. Sources C and D show that they once believed in other goddesses too. But we know very little about them.

Great heroes and legendary creatures

The Anglo-Saxons believed in great heroes, like gods. They also believed in witches, monsters and demons.

Stories about gods and imaginary people and creatures are called **myths**, or legends.

Weland the smith

One Anglo-Saxon hero was named Weland the smith. He was believed to be a magical blacksmith. Once he was made a prisoner by Nidhad, one of his enemies. But he escaped. He was linked to ancient burial mounds. Christian writers, years later, had heard of him.

Giants and choosers of the dead

Anglo-Saxons also believed in giants. They thought giants must have built the Roman cities, now in ruins. Anglo-Saxons also believed in female spirits who decided which warriors would die in battle. This was the best way for a warrior to die. Their name means 'choosers of the dead', in **Old English**. Later Vikings called them Valkyries.

Source A

Cities are seen from afar, cunning work of giants.

An Anglo-Saxon poem describes a ruined Roman city, possibly Bath.

Source B

Where now are the bones of the wise and well known smith Weland?

Written by King Alfred of Wessex, in about AD890.

Source C

This is an ancient burial mound in Oxfordshire. It is called Wayland's (Weland's) Smithy. This name is first recorded in AD955.

Dragons and monsters

Treasure hoards were guarded by dragons and monsters. Anglo-Saxon myths tell of a hero called Beowulf. He killed two of these monsters and a dragon.

Elves

Anglo-Saxons also believed in magical creatures called elves. They were like fairies. There were many different kinds:

- mountain elves.
- wood elves.
- field elves.
- wild elves.
- sea elves.
- hill elves

In poems lovely women were sometimes called 'beautiful as an elf'.

How do we know?

Source B shows that Christians, like King Alfred, knew all about Weland. Source C shows that people linked his name to an old burial mound. Perhaps they thought he lived there.

Source A shows that people believed in giants. Some were thought to build cities.

Sons of the gods

Anglo-Saxon kings believed they were descended from gods, who had been the first members of their families.

Sons of Woden

Anglo-Saxon kings thought they were different from other people. They were members of a royal family. There is a special **Old English** word for royal family. It is 'cyning'. The modern word 'king' comes from this.

The rulers had believed this long before they came to Britain. They thought that some families were more important than other ones. Lists were made of the kings of a kingdom. They were supposed to all be from the same family. The first king on the list was usually Woden. He was the warrior god. Even after the Anglo-Saxons became Christians they still kept these lists.

Sons of Seaxnet

One kingdom claimed its kings came from a different god. This was the kingdom of the East Saxons. Here they thought the god Seaxnet was the first king. We do not know why they chose him instead of Woden.

Source A

They choose their kings according to their families. They choose their generals according to their courage.

The Roman Tacitus wrote this about German tribes. He wrote in the first century AD. Among these tribes were Anglo-Saxons before they came to Britain.

Source B

Seaxnet
Gesecg
Antsecg
Swaeppa
Sigefugl
Bedca
Offa
Aescwine
Sledda

A list of the kings of the East Saxons (Essex).

They were the sons of Wictgils, whose father was Witta, whose father was Wecta, son of Woden. From him came the royal families of many kingdoms.

*Written by the Anglo-Saxon Bede, in about AD731. He is describing the **ancestors** of Hengest, first king of Kent.*

A list of kings who ruled in England. It says they started from Woden. The picture is of Woden. This was made in the 13th century AD.

How do we know?

Source A shows that the idea that gods were ancestors of kings was an old one. It was believed even before the first Anglo-Saxons came to Britain.

Source C shows that Anglo-Saxons thought the god Woden had started their royal families. But Source B shows that the East Saxons were different. We do not know why.

Source D shows that even after Christianity replaced the old beliefs, the lists of kings were still kept.

Temples and sacrifices

We know that the Anglo-Saxons had special places where they worshipped their gods. But we know very little about these places.

Temples of the gods

The Anglo-Saxons had special places where they **worshipped** their gods. We know about them because:

* They were mentioned by later Christian Anglo-Saxons, writing about the earlier **pagan** religions.

* Some place-names show temples were once there. Some contain the Old English word 'hearg'. This means a temple. Some contain 'weoh'. This means holy place.

None of these temples has been found by **archaeologists**. They may have been wooden huts. Or they may have been just clearings in woods. We know though that they probably had statues of gods in them. Perhaps these were statues of animals worshipped as gods. We cannot be sure. Some **British**, who were still pagans, would have worshipped them. But the British Christians thought these were bad things. They called them **idols**.

Source A

Places where once the crude pillars of the foul snake and the stag were worshipped stupidly in wicked shrines.

Written by the Christian Anglo-Saxon, Aldhelm. He died in AD710. The people he described might have been British pagans as well as Anglo-Saxon ones.

Source B

They always sacrifice one in ten of their prisoners before sailing home.

The Roman writer Sidonius Apollinaris wrote this, about Anglo-Saxon raiders in Europe, in the fifth century AD.

Source C

The eleventh month was called Blotmonath. ['blood-month'] It means month of sacrifices.

Written by the Christian Anglo-Saxon, Bede. He died in AD735.

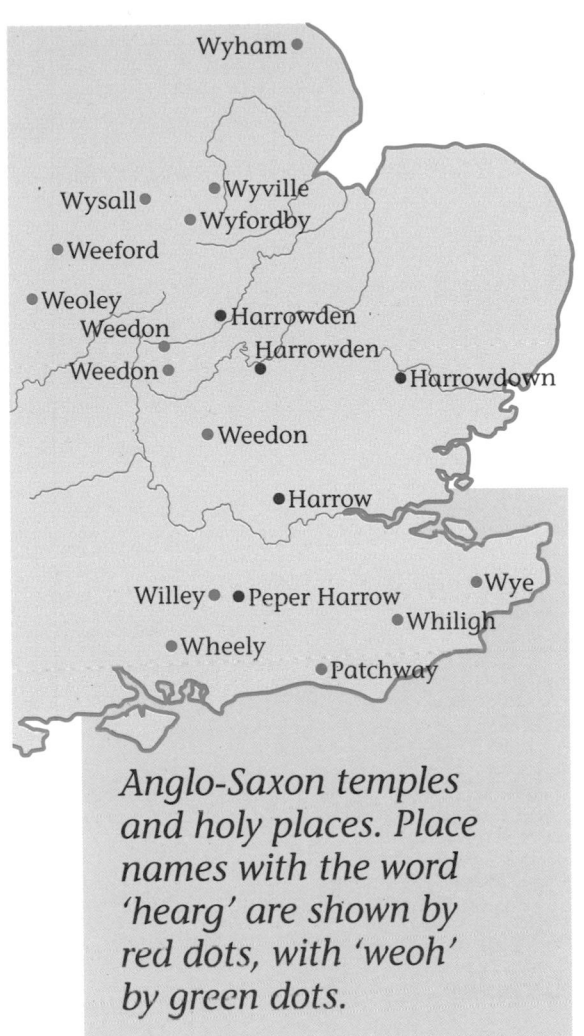

Anglo-Saxon temples and holy places. Place names with the word 'hearg' are shown by red dots, with 'weoh' by green dots.

Sacrifices

The pagan Anglo-Saxons killed animals and gave them to their gods. This is called a **sacrifice**. One of the months of their year was a special time for killing animals in this way.

Human sacrifices?

Roman writers thought Anglo-Saxon raiders also sacrificed people. There are **British** writers, too, who thought they sometimes killed helpless people. These may have been sacrifices too.

At Sutton Hoo in Suffolk some bodies were found which might have been sacrifices. One man was buried with a plough. This might have been done to ask the gods to make the crops grow. We cannot be sure.

How do we know?

Source A shows that statues of animals were sometimes worshipped by pagan Anglo-Saxons.

Source C shows that pagan Anglo-Saxons sacrificed to their gods. Source B shows such sacrifices have included people. This may have happened in Britain, too.

Spells, charms and magic

Some Anglo-Saxons tried to use magic to change their lives and make things happen.

Magic is trying to make things happen by saying spells or charms. **Pagan** Anglo-Saxons believed in magic. Christians did not. But even when they joined the Christians, some Anglo-Saxons still tried to make things happen by magic.

Charms

Charms are special words or rhymes. They were used to make crops grow better. They were used to keep people safe. Anglo-Saxons thought that gods, elves or witches might try to harm them. They used charms to protect themselves.

Stones and trees

Some Anglo-Saxons thought they could cure illnesses by going to special stones or trees. They thought they had magical powers.

Runes

The first Anglo-Saxons in Britain had their own special way of writing. These letters were called runes. Some people thought that they were magical. They used them to make magic spells. Some runes were put on pots. Some were put on weapons.

Source A

If it were shot [attacks] of the gods, or shot of the elves, or shot of the haegtessan now I will help you. May the Lord help you.

An Anglo-Saxon charm, tenth century AD, to protect against sickness or bad luck. By then Anglo-Saxons were Christians. This is why the Lord Jesus is mentioned in the last line. But some still kept on believing in old charms.

Source B

Men are such fools. They will bring offerings to stone, or tree, or spring. The dead stone and the dumb tree.

The Christian Anglo-Saxon, Elfric wrote this in the eleventh century AD.

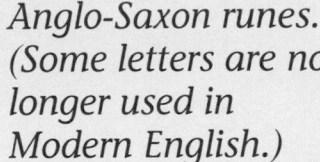

Runes carved on a knife, found at Battersea, London.

Anglo-Saxon runes. (Some letters are no longer used in Modern English.)

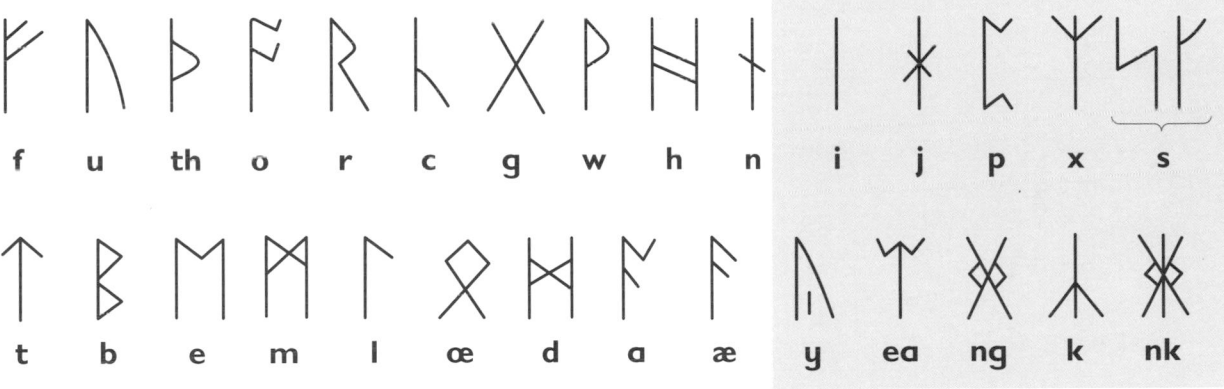

f u th o r c g w h n   i j p x s

t b e m l œ ð a æ   y ea ng k nk

Crystal balls

Many crystal balls have been found in pagan Anglo-Saxon graves. They are mostly found in the graves of women. They may have been thought to have had magical powers. Anglo-Saxons thought that some women had magic powers. A woman like this was called a heahrune. Wicked women who worked magic were called 'haegtessan', which means 'witch'. The modern word 'hag' comes from this. Men could be witches as well as women.

How do we know?

Source A shows that charms were used to protect people from attacks called shots.

Source B shows some people thought some stones, trees and springs had magic powers. Most Christians thought this was wrong. Source C shows that runes were sometimes put on objects. We do not know why.

The coming of Christianity

In AD597 Christian preachers came from Rome to the Anglo-Saxon kingdom of Kent. Soon Anglo-Saxons began to believe in Jesus. The Christian religion spead across England.

Later Anglo-Saxons told a story about how **Pope** Gregory in Rome had first met Anglo-Saxons. They had been slaves in Rome. He decided to send **missionaries** to Britain to tell the Anglo-Saxons about Christianity.

Augustine comes to Kent

The first Christian missionaries were led by a man named Augustine. The Anglo-Saxon king of Kent at the time was named Ethelbert. He had married a Christian princess from what is now France. Ethelbert was a **pagan**.

Ethelbert allowed the Christians to use an old Roman church in Canterbury. This was the church of St Martin. Before long, Ethelbert himself had joined the Christians. He persuaded the king of the East Saxons (Essex) to become a Christian too. Many Anglo-Saxon people followed their kings and became Christians. They may have also been encouraged by **British** Christians, who had been conquered by the Anglo-Saxons.

Source A

'What is the name of these people?' he asked. 'They are called Angles,' he was told. 'That's a good name,' he said, 'for they have faces like angels. And it is right that they should share heaven with the angels.'

A story of how Pope Gregory first met Anglo-Saxon slaves in Rome, in the late sixth century AD. The story was written by the Anglo-Saxon, Bede, in about AD731. He said the story had been told for many years.

Christians from Scotland

Not all Christian missionaries were sent to the Anglo-Saxons by the Pope in Rome. Some came from the Picts and Scots, who lived in what is now Scotland. Here there was an important **monastery** at Iona. Christian ideas spread from Iona to the kingdoms of Northumbria, Mercia and Essex. In AD663 a meeting was held in Whitby, Northumbria. At this meeting most of the Christians in Britain agreed to accept the Pope in Rome as their leader in spiritual things.

Source B

Ruins of an early Anglo-Saxon Christian church in Kent. It was built around a Roman building. This is the brick part in the middle. The Roman building may also have been a church.

Trouble between the old and new beliefs

Christianity spread across Anglo-Saxon England. But at times there was trouble between it and the old pagan beliefs.

After AD597 the Anglo-Saxon kingdoms gradually became Christian. People began to give up their **pagan** beliefs.

The spread of Christianity

King Edwin of Northumbria became a Christian in AD627 and the chief priest of the old pagan religion accepted Christianity and destroyed a pagan temple. King Cynegils of Wessex became a Christian in AD635. Peada, son of the king of Mercia, did the same in AD653.

Trouble with the old beliefs

Christians thought the pagan beliefs were wrong. They thought the old gods were evil. But some pagans opposed the new idea that there was only one God.

King Redwald of East Anglia tried to worship both Jesus and the old gods. When he died, in AD625, he was buried in the way that pagans thought was right, with all his treasure in a burial mound.

Source A

Then, full of joy at his knowledge of the worship of the true God, he told his companions to set fire to the temple.

How the chief priest of the Northumbrian pagans turned against the old gods in AD627. This was written by Bede in about AD731.

Source B

He stood in front of the pagans on a high mound. He tried to curse the people of God. He tried to control them by the use of **magic**.

How the chief priest of the South Saxons (Sussex) opposed a group of Christians led by Wilfrid. This happened in AD666.

Source C

The **idols** are to be destroyed. But the temples are to be made clean with holy water.

A letter from Pope Gregory to Mellitus in AD601. Mellitus was a Christian in England.

Source D

Archaeologists digging up the boat in which Redwald of East Anglia was probably buried. The boat and the treasure show that this king was buried in a pagan way.

When Sabert, the first Christian king of Essex, died in about AD616 his people began **worshipping** the old pagan gods again. This happened in Kent and in Northumbria too. Later, all these kingdoms became Christian.

In Sussex the chief pagan led the people against Christians. Christian kings made laws to stop the pagan beliefs. But people sometimes turned back to the old gods in times of trouble. This happened in Essex, in AD664 during a plague.

How do we know?

Source A shows that in Northumbria the chief pagan helped the first Christians. But Source B shows that in Sussex the chief pagan was against the Christians. Source C shows that Christians used old pagan temples to worship God in. Source D shows how one Anglo-Saxon king kept on following the old pagan ways, even though he said he was a Christian.

Anglo-Saxon Christian churches

As Christianity spread, the Anglo-Saxons began to build churches across England.

Preaching crosses

In many areas the first Christians had no churches. Instead stone crosses were set up at meeting places. Here Christian preachers told people about God. Some of these people would have been new Anglo-Saxon Christians. Some would have been British people, whose families had been Christian since Roman times.

The first churches

The first churches were often built of wood. When King Edwin of Northumbria became a Christian, in AD627, he was **baptised** in a small wooden church at York.

Some churches were built where Roman Christians had **worshipped** God. Others were built where **pagan** temples had been. Others were built where famous Christians were buried.

Building with stone

By the tenth century AD more and more churches were being built out of stone. These were the biggest buildings most people would ever see. They usually had a cemetery around them, where the dead were buried. Kings made people give money to help pay for the churches.

Stone preaching cross from Eyam, Derbyshire. Probably made in the eighth century AD.

Source D

Stone tower of Earls Barton church, Northamptonshire. Built in the tenth century AD.

How do we know?

Source A shows that the first Christians often met at a stone cross. Source C is one of these crosses.

Source D shows that churches were built from stone in the tenth century. Source B shows that kings made people pay money to the Church.

Monks and nuns

Some Anglo-Saxons lived in Christian communities, worshipping God.

Monks were men and nuns were women who had decided to spend their lives worshipping God. They did not marry. Instead they lived in groups of people of the same sex. They gave up their possessions. This was seen as a holy way to live. Kings and nobles often gave rich gifts to these communities. They thought that God would be pleased with them for helping holy people.

Making beautiful objects

Monks and nuns were skilled at writing. They wrote out copies of the Bible and prayer books by hand. They decorated them richly. They also made lovely objects from gold and silver for use in church.

Changes in the tenth century

In the tenth century, some **Church** leaders felt that monks and nuns should live much holier lives. People were shocked by the way they were behaving. Monks were sent abroad to find out about the Rule of Saint Benedict. This Rule gave strict instructions how monks and nuns should live. It said that they should eat very plain food, and not much of it. It said when they should pray, and how many

Source A

Finely decorated cloth given to monks by King Athelstan in AD934. It was to be put in the grave of Saint Cuthbert, a holy monk who had died nearly 250 years before.

church services they should attend every day. New monasteries were started which followed the Rule of St Benedict.

Source B

A page of a book made by Winchester monks in AD980. It shows an angel talking to women at Christ's empty tomb.

How do we know?

Source A shows that kings gave rich gifts to monks.

Source B shows that monks and nuns were skilled at making beautiful books.

Source C tells us that a monk was sent abroad to find out about new ideas laying down how monks should live.

Source C

Learn how to live the way the Rule says. Then teach it to the other monks back home.

Instructions given to a monk in about AD955. He was sent to what is now France to learn the Rule of St Benedict.

Places of the dead

Some pagan Anglo-Saxons burned the bodies of the dead. Others buried them unburned.

North of the river Thames most pagan people burnt the dead. This is called **cremation**. South of the Thames most buried their dead unburned.

Cremations and pots

Burnt bones and ashes were usually buried in pots. Rich people sometimes used bronze dishes. Poorer people used bags.

Perhaps people thought that by burning the body they freed the person's spirit. Archaeologists have found that about one pot in every ten has a hole drilled in it. Could this have been to let the spirit out? The burned bones in the pots came mainly from skulls and the top of a person's body. Perhaps people thought this was where a person's spirit lived.

Tiny razors and combs were sometimes put in the pots. This shows people thought that the head was an important part of a person's body. Sometimes mounds were piled up over the pots. Sometimes there were wooden buildings over the buried pots.

Source A

The dragon shall be in the burial mound – the dragon is old and rich in treasure.

An early Anglo-Saxon poem from the Exeter Book.

Source B

Burnt remains of bronze brooches. These were found in a pot holding cremated bones. The pot was found at Loveden Hill, in Lincolnshire. The burial dates from about AD500.

26

Source C

Things buried with an unburned body and found at Sarre, in Kent. They are from the sixth century AD.

Unburned bodies

Weapons, jewellery and pots were buried with unburned bodies. These may have been for people to use in the next world. Or they may have been meant to show how important people were when they were alive. The custom grew more common during the sixth century. Mounds of earth were piled up over rich graves. But the Saxons believed the buried treasure was safe because it was guarded by dragons.

Horsemeat was sometimes buried with men, and both men and women were buried with joints of beef. Meat seems never to have been put into children's graves. Nuts, fruits and eggs were buried with men, women and children. Perhaps this food was meant for the next life. We can only guess why different foods were put with different people.

How do we know?

Source C shows rich objects were sometimes buried with unburnt bodies. Source A shows people thought dragons would guard treasure like this. Source B shows things were buried with cremated people too. But they were often burned with the body, so it is hard to see exactly what they were.

Changing ideas about death

The coming of Christianity changed the way people buried the dead. But the changes are not always easy to understand.

Bodies without belongings

During the seventh century AD some people began to bury their dead without any belongings. This was probably because Christians believed dead people could not take things to heaven. By the eighth century few people were buried with belongings. But very holy people were sometimes still buried with rich objects.

Rich burials under mounds

Not everyone in the seventh century agreed with the Christian way of doing things. In some areas treasure was buried with dead people under mounds. Graves like these have been found at Sutton Hoo in Suffolk, Taplow in Buckinghamshire, in the Peak District of Derbyshire and in Wiltshire.

Perhaps they were the graves of **pagans** trying to oppose the spread of Christianity. At Sutton Hoo there seem to have been human **sacrifices** linked to the burial.

Source A

*A cross buried with the Northumbrian Christian, Cuthbert. He was a very holy man who died in AD687. Some rich objects were put in his coffin in AD698. This was when people began to treat him as a **saint**. Much later, some more things were put in his coffin.*

L.HL85
1175-7

N
↑

Graves from Lechlade in Gloucestershire. Sixth century graves face north-south. Seventh century graves face east-west.

Changing ways of digging graves

Christians dug graves facing from east to west. This way of digging graves became more common during the seventh century. This may show how Christian ideas changed people's habits. But some Anglo-Saxon pagans had done this before. So we cannot be certain the change was always due to Christians. We do know that people were buried in a Christian way from the eighth century on, because the Church made rules about how this should be done.

Cemeteries around churches

During the eighth and ninth centuries AD more and more churches were built. After this time dead people were buried round these Christian churches.

How do we know?

Source B shows that people changed the way they dug graves. This happened during the seventh century AD. But we cannot be sure the change was always caused by new Christian beliefs. Source A shows that some very holy Christian people were still buried with rich objects. This was to show them respect.

Glossary

archaeologists people who dig up and study things made in the past

ancestor a member of your family who has been dead for a long time

baptise people are baptised with water, when they join the Christian Church

barbarians tribes from outside the Roman Empire

British people living in Britain before the Anglo-Saxons came

charms words or objects supposed to keep the owner safe, by magic

cremation burning dead bodies

Church the organization that made the rules for Christians

idol statue of a pagan god, or goddess

magic doing or saying things like spells to make things happen

missionaries people who take the Christian message to other countries

monastery place where monks or nuns live

monks men who spend their lives worshipping God, keeping away from things that might distract them. Women who live like this are called nuns.

myth a story about the gods or imaginary people, to explain things about the world. Also called a **legend**.

Old English the language of the Anglo-Saxons

pagans the Christians' name for people who worshipped different gods

Pope leader of the Christian Church in western Europe

sacrifice giving something to God, or the gods

saints people who lived such holy lives that they were prayed to after they had died

sheaf a bunch of wheat, or corn

shrine a special place which is thought to be holy

Vikings people from Denmark and Norway who attacked Britain after AD789

worship praising and showing respect to God, or the gods